W9-AOZ-881

Happy
Moms
Day !!
:)

Love you!
Joe, Michelle
Sarah & Carly
Sam

To

....

From

....

When God
Created Mothers

WHEN GOD CREATED MOTHERS
Copyright © 2005 by the Estate of Erma Bombeck. All rights reserved.

ISBN-10: 0-7407-5108-5
ISBN-13: 978-0-7407-5108-0

07 08 09 RR6 10 9 8 7 6 5 4 3 2

Illustrations by Lynn Chang

When God Created Mothers

by
ERMA BOMBECK

**Andrews McMeel
Publishing**

Kansas City

W hen the good Lord was creating mothers, He was into His **sixth** day of overtime when the angel appeared and said, "You're doing a lot of

fiddling

around on this one."

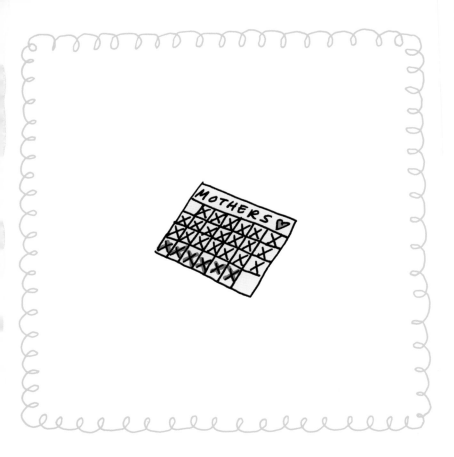

And the Lord said,
"Have you read the specs
on this order?

"She has to be ***completely* washable, but not plastic;**

"Have

180

movable parts . . .

all replaceable;

"Run on
black coffee
and leftovers;

"Have a lap
that **disappears**
when she stands up;

"A kiss that can cure anything from a broken leg to a disappointed love affair;

"And **six** pairs of hands."

The angel
shook her head s l o w l y
and said,

"*Six* pairs of hands?
No way."

"It's not the hands that are causing me problems," said the Lord. "It's the three pairs of *eyes* that mothers have to have."

"That's on the standard model?" asked the angel.

The Lord nodded.
"One pair that sees through
closed doors when she asks,

'What are you kids
doing in there?'

when she already knows.

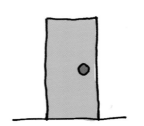

Another *here*

in the **back** of her head

that sees what she *shouldn't*

but what she **has** to know,

and of course the ones
here in front that can look at
a child when he goofs up and say,

'I understand and I love you,'

without so much as uttering
a word."

"Lord," said the angel,
        touching His sleeve gently,
    "come to bed. Tomorrow—"

    "I can't," said the Lord.
"I'm so close to creating something
        so close to myself. Already I have
one who heals herself
        when she is sick . . .

can feed a family of **six**

on **one pound**

of hamburger . . .

and
can
get a
nine-year-old
to
stand
under
a
shower."

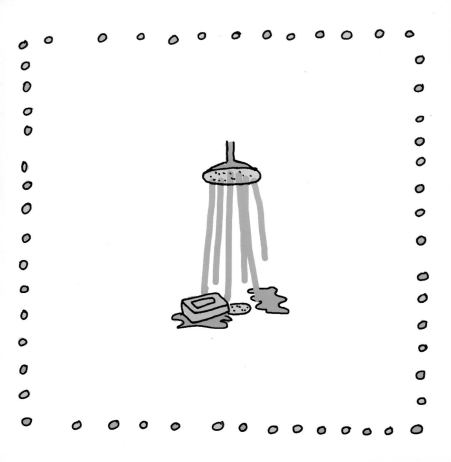

The angel circled the model of a mother very slowly.

"It's too soft," she sighed.

"But tough!"
said the Lord excitedly.
"You cannot imagine what
this mother can do or endure."

"Can it *think?*"

"Not only **think,**
but it can reason
and compromise,"

said the Creator.

Finally the angel bent over
and ran her finger across the cheek.

"There's a **leak**," she pronounced.
"I told you that you were trying to put
too much into this model."

"It's not a leak," said the Lord.
"It's a *tear*."

"What's it for?"

"It's for **joy**, *sadness*, disappointment, **pain**, *loneliness* and **pride**."

"You are a **genius**," said the angel.

The Lord looked s o m b e r.
"**I** didn't put it there."